"...A LOVELY SLICF ... "

Typeset and Published
by
The National Poetry Foundation
(Reg Charity No 283032)
27 Mill Rd
Fareham
Hants PO16 0TH
(Tel: 0329 822218)

Printed by
Meon Valley Printers
Bishops Waltham (0489 895460)

First published 1991
Reprinted (with corrections) 1992

Sponsored by Rosemary Arthur

Cover Photograph by Celia Rambaut

Back cover photo courtesy of Farmer's Weekly Magazine

'Christmas Morning', from which the title of this book is taken, and which comes from Spike Milligan's book *The Bedside Milligan*, is reproduced with the kind permission of the author.

Previous publications: "Requiem for Innocence" 1990.

Alan's work has also appeared in *Orbis, Otter, Staple, Pause, New Prospect Poetry* and *Farmer's Weekly*, been accepted by *The Countryman*, and been featured by BBC Radio and TV.

ISBN 1 870556 41 0

£4.00

CHRISTMAS MORNING

A little girl called Silé Javotte
Said, "look at the lovely presents I've got."
A little girl in Biafra said,
"Oh! What a lovely slice of bread."

Spike Milligan

For Pat, 1991

CONTENTS

***

POETRY CIRCLE

We like the sounds the pictures paint.
Sly passion throbs beyond restraint
Coy patience curls in words unstressed
We love the smell of anaepests,

From time to time we find the lines
Smoothe rhythms of the semi–rhymes
Milk tension from a harsh quatrain,
Curse the scansion that will not scan.

But when it all is said and done
We really only like the fun
Of hearing other people's views
And catching up on local news.

FRUSTRATION

J said, "Write on frustration
In a relationship." Jim would.
I have gone off him. Right off.
I've never really thought beyond
Frustrations. The heat and anger.
I don't need reasons. Reason flies
Out of the windows with the crockery
And the furniture. Now discussion is
Different. Discussions are all right.
It's when he won't see. He won't see.
He doesn't even try to see. I want
To write about fluffy chicks and
Little baby ducks and girls on
Thistledown lying in the sun.
I don't want to write about
Frustration and anger. I'm
A bit cross about it. Fact
I'm bloody Livid. Surely he
Knew that I like beauty. He
Should have known that I like
Rainbows. Clouds lit from below
And colour wash on hills. Impasto
Rocks in bracken. Frustration? Why
Go on and on insisting? Hell! Knowing
Yet he persisted, "Write on Frustration
In a relationship." I won't do it. No. No
I'll tell him, "I'm not even going to
Try to write it."

FLASHFLOOD

A not quite time before the night,
when roofs lean in above sepulchral streets
and walls advance in palisades of dark. Watcher,
I shelter in a deeper dark.

A Kafka world.
Carved images of lampost light.
Blind shadows. Icons
stamped out, hard
silhouettes
against fluorescence
of a chippie shop.

Fears;
Pooh–sticks between reflections,
aquaplane, spatter
a brolly carapace.
Umbral forms congeal
wait, wet–foot
curse wakes, non–stop
coaches
come and go.
Wind catches flotsam in its arms
and dances by
with salt and vinegar on its breath.

Such rain.
The raven world is washed.
In lambent airs
the dove does not return.

STORM MORNING

Anvil clouds disguise a glowering night,
dark silence wraps the smuggled hint of day
before sharp lightening rips a pregnant dawn
and thunder cries the labour pangs of light.
The waters break, a crystal day is born;
spring sun is crowned to heady scent of may
and birdsong anthems crowing dawn's delight.

PATH

Our lane,
rutted by passing,
rambles
between primroses
and fields
cable stitched
by ploughs.

Cool leaves sift
sunlight,
golden flour
dust
slow-march of cows
milk-heavy,
black on white
like moving negatives.

A kestrel quarters,
hovers
crucified
against a cloud.

EXMOOR HALF-LIGHT

Last year I sat on snag-tooth rock
By Twichen Ridge, by Western Ball,
To paint the dying of the light.
As sleepy day-life slipped to peace
A drowsing sun drew down the blinds,
Quiet as ebb of Saunton seas
Mounted the night-light sentry stars
To watch it sleep day-dreams away.

There, Exford lay cocooned in crepe
There Molland, swathed in bombazine,
Beyond, I saw North Molton weep
Reflect South Molton's distant grief
Assuaged with crimson neon tears.
Cold-crescent moon woke, button-bright,
And last-light drained from Horsen Hill
In wash of purple heather glaze.

As colours greyed I watched the sky
Sigh widow-weeds around the moor;
Where wake winds keen in crevassed crags,
And darkness wakes unshriven ghosts
To moan the mournful moorland dirge;
Wild music drawn by eldritch choirs
Who summon Death from heathland graves
By wind-whipped, piping buzzard call.

By Withypool the piper pranced
Hopped peak to peak across the Chains,
Whirled iron age dust from Butter Mill
To douse the flame at Dunkery.
Playing the tune we all must call
Round circled stones at Hawkcombe Head,
Set free the dancing deathless souls
To ghost–write stories in the dew.

HOLIDAY 2000

Yes, holidays in Devon are the best.
You drive along the new road hub to hub
Until the sign, in day-glow, "Cum'n Rest"
Beside a horse-plough and a dead oak's stub.
They boast, 'The Finest Camping In The West'
And call themselves, 'The Moorland Vista Club'.
The tents go on for miles in line abreast

And over there the caravans belay
On little concrete pads by lines of flowers;
Just over there's the games room and café,
Across the yard the you-know-what and showers.

A painted notice says, "*And this means you.*
Keep to the paths." (You know, they're all the same.)
"*Please do not use the sand-pit as a loo.*
Keep off the trees - Please use the climbing frame.
Please do not pick the flowers." There's lots to do.
"*Play on the slides and swings. Enjoy a game.*
Keep off the grass. To golf - Please form a queue."

You must not walk your dog down by the boats
In case he soils the stretch of silver sand
Or paddles in the sea where sewage floats
And flotsam condoms decorate the strand.

Of course, their 'Pleasure–drome' has got the lot;
Just up the road, beyond the camping site,
There's everything you need, right on the spot.
There's fish and chips, arcades, and neon light
And bars and clubs where everyone's on pot
And there is disco dancing every night.
Some think, 'The Living Country World' is rot

They've got a cow called Blossom and a pig,
Three ducks, a sheep, a donkey and a hen.
They stink like hell, but well, the kids can twig
What proper country's like – just now and then.

INCOMERS

We thought "Country will be heaven"
we thought city life is hell
so we bought a barn in Devon
and converted it. It's swell.
There's a plaque to Ernie Bevin
and, my dear, we've got a well.

We joined the snooty country clubs
avoided common locals
we did not use the village pubs
we found them full of yokels
who pointedly ignored our snubs
and sang rude rustic vocals.

Every Sunday at eleven
they ring changes, practice peals,
they milk bloody cows at seven
drive huge tractors in the fields,
and the piglets in their shippen
squeal those paralysing squeals.

As you know, we're 'All Organic'
but we said we'd have no truck,
– my poor hubby went quite manic –
with the farmer spreading muck,
and we quite enjoyed the panic
when the salmonella struck.

We complained about the farmer
we complained about the muck,
we complained about the church bells
but without a lot of luck;
for they told us where to put them
– and our solitary duck.

Well, it's not what we expected;
we demand change, as our right,
and we seem to be respected,
people seem to be polite
but it seems we're not *accepted*
in this pastoral delight.

EXMOOR NIGHT WATCH

Midnight and moorbreath. Hangley Cleve.
The guardian challenge of the owl.
Spectres that coil in brittle glow,
Soft, silvered sighs from phantom forms,
Congealing, blurring time and place
Release imagination's flight
To magic worlds: to make believe
Where fancy flies on spirit wings.

From cobweb, cashmere shawls of mist
Ghost–ships, beyond the White Post hedge,
Sail, silent, mew to sweatered ewes,
Confirm the gentle mewl of lambs
And anchor, to the rip of grass.
On black–night steeds with moon–flame breath
Apocalyptic horsemen ride,
Circling, menace and dissolve.

Now, all around, the hussif wraiths
Dance roundelays with shepherd boys.
'Gentlemen' ride against the stage
Or grin on gibbets, sway and twist
To face the final cardinals.
Ghost Carver rides through Higher Ball
To Simonsbath and on to Oare
And back to grieve in Badgworthy.

From Ferny Ball, from Sandyway
Sad, crying ghosts of regal stags
Sweep by with terror on their breath.
Harsh, spirit hunt–horns bray to vaunt

Hunters hollooing, *Kill to save.*
Conserving hound-packs swirl and swoop,
Leave spirals in the knife-sharp air
To banner valour of the chase.

In pride of place, on walls of bars,
Sad multitudes of hat-stand royals
Acclaim the courage of the knights
Who slay the dragon herbivore.
Dog-collared men, revered in pink,
Who extol prayer and genuflect
Uncalloused knees then, saddle sore,
Preach of compassion - gone away.

Darkly, in some miasmic gorge
Excited pleasure seekers meet
At bearpit, or to bait the bull,
Laugh at the spectral badger dig,
Wring the blinded cockerel's neck,
Or drop the dogs on barrelled rats;
Jack Russells bred by Sporty Jack.
Loved fun 'e did, did Parson Jack.

The moor in heady scented dark
Winnows the mind, dispels the dross,
Shows in the midnight mirror truth;
Raw bones without the flesh of lies.
Snail-trails of lust beneath the stone
Highlight the cant behind the smile.
Cruelty lives beneath the rock,
Breeds in this wild, harsh, savage place.

SHEEP DIPPING

To calls, "Eradicate the scab", they
fall in line and dip the head, face front
at tension stand, prick eared, to rally cries
that promise greener fields. They follow
where the lead sheep leads, the Judas
with security, that walks scot free and
when the cold douche comes, stands back
and bleats; derides the cure and blames
the shepherd who prescribed the remedy.

BROILER PICNIC

Progress has solved the problem. At last
the quail is saved – intensively – and,
like its chicken cousins, constantly protected
from a world where nature rules.

Under neon suns computers rule, control
a world of ordered lives and constant purity, and
monitor the scale of ordered deaths to meet
the constant deadline.

Spitted above charcoal and the Harrod's box
they turn, constantly, and hiss small bursts of flame
on red hot coals. The picnic ends, bones powder,
spiral, freely, in a puff of wind.

A recent report in a newspaper stated that problems associated with intensive rearing of quails have, at last, been solved.

OUT OF MILK

In thirty years he'd had enough.
"Get out of milk," friends said,
"Enough's enough." A life's time, timed
each five o'clock of every day
to feed and clean and milk his herd.

In numbered lots he sold his cows, all named
and individual; Lot 1. Old Buttercup, Lot 2. Her calf,
Lot 3. Black Maisey with the crooked teat,
then white-face Tinkerbell who kicked, and
trusting Bess who stretched to nuzzle him.

The booted buyers came from everywhere;
calculating, know-how men with knowing thumbs
that poked and prodded carcass value to a T,
or hands that stroked an udder to the final cent.
At dusk he totalled columns as the last truck left.

Next day he rose at five o'clock. In silent sheds
smoothed rails of empty cubicles, remembered
parlour smells of dung, companionship and warmth,
soft sough of feet, the clicking of machines
and had to shout to hear the silence break.

Shaving, he thought of Buttercup and Bell,
and longed to feel the muzzle silk of Bess.
He weighed the cost against the price of trust
and could not meet accusing eyes, beyond the steam,
that watched him from the mirror on the wall.

THE BULL

I have no God, for I am Beast, yet
I could crush you with my knee, or
gut you like a fish, with no more effort
than to break a blade of grass or flick a fly.
From strength I swallow pride,
allow a child to lead me,
turn the other cheek, assume a deafness
to your curse. In retribution
I do not seek an eye, nor answer blow with blow,
yet I could crush you if I would.
My life, you price in coats or shoes
or washers for a tap, careless hang me
naked on the butcher-hook, the prey to 'Man'
who kneel, praise God, read truths
from vellum pasted with my bones, cull parables
from scriptures bound in hide. I am Beast.
I have no God of mercy, yet
I could crush you – if I would.

THERE MUST BE A REASON

L'Abbey de Senanque,
To scents of pine and lavender,
Holds chants to God and silences
Of equal worth. Within stone walls
A harsh essential must ferments
Where millennial still distils
A calm spirit.

Tourists, we call,
Pay voyeur fees, weigh daily doubts
Against their certain sanctuary.
Their faith demands an awesome trust
Their minima provide such surety.
We come to wonder how
And why.

No sign of weakness there.
From where I sit, numbed
By drone and hard oak,
He soars against stained glass
Crucified, above the Cross.
Weighed with the Word
His brazen glare transfixes me
Unblinking, ruthless. Talons
Prick the globe of conscience, wait
To snatch an unsuspecting mouse of sin.

NORTH DEVON FULL CIRCLE

A granite doorpost of the empty home of God
carved by a stone–aged mason from the dawn of time.
Stone Age concentric circles in a doom day slab
from Sacred Altars the evangelists defiled.

The Christian era tripped the ego path;
saints smashing Nympton and the Nymet shrines
brought signal message from the only God
to Holy Places of the pagan Celt.

It preached of sacrificial love of church;
condemned the sacrilege of simple faith;
a love of gods of springtime, sun and rain
of Sacred Waters, harvest, hope and lust.

Omnipotent, its acolytes sought tithes,
taught hell and sin (and absolution's price),
forgiving praised the power of love: as proof
killed Becket in a 'proper' Holy Place.

These true believers came. To expiate
– and stamp the passport to eternal peace –
built churches as the second homes of God
from ruined altars of another Truth.

Full circle turn, the godless rites prevail
where Hope and Faith are just grandmother's names,
the penance church is now a bingo hall
and good intentions drown in lifeless leets.

Carved, patterned icon from an ancient Grove
Salvation's granite record of a sacred trust
encrusted relict pilfered from a Pagan site;
concentric circles spiralled by the Christian act.

The names Nymet, Nimet and Nympton found in Devon date from pre-Christian times and were sites of pagan 'Sacred Groves', often associated with rivers or streams. Early Christian missionaries, notably Martin of Tours, came and destroyed these Sacred Groves. (He was duly canonised!) Recently a granite doorpost in the church at Broadnimet was found to have pre-Christian carvings of concentric circles on it, which certainly came from such a place.

William de Tracy, one of the four knights who murdered Thomas à Becket, fled to Devon and, as penance, built several churches in the area. There is a carved head in the porch of Nymet Tracey church which is said to represent him.

ROCK FALL

There is the ruin of the church
A granite remnant of a darkling truth.
Cathedrals, built on faith and rock,
Would prick the sky when man could reach
No higher than his finger tips. Then
Luminescent priests conjuring Hell, promised
By prayer and tithe and candled fear,
A priceless heaven for the poor; praising penury
Priced absolution and the bones of saints.

Today, we fly beyond the stars. Storm tossed
In wisdom–broken worlds of broken words,
We find no promised God, no promised Heaven.
We do not choose to hear the quarter–vicar plead,
His voice drowned out by rabble–babble chants
Where virtue is excess of sin. Now
Piety will buy no match to set the flame,
Nor purgatory show a candle's light
Beneath the roof of trust that leaks.

SKY PILOT

He and the taloned eagle bear the Word,
and prey to clutch both this world
and the next. Beneath their feet
the congregation hunts; hawk-eyed
peeps between the praying hands
to quarter virtue's field.
Smothered in sermon, pew-bound, fancy
freed to fly the Amen bombing run
on Satan and that dreadful Mrs. Smith.

Warm in the love of God and freed from sin
they gather at the graveyard edge, then swoop
to claw the secret vices of a lesser friend
and smile to watch a small world fall apart.

FOR GODS' SAKE

I hate the infidel
Who does not see
The God I know,
Who teaches me, that
I am not as other men,
But safe, in virtue,
In his care.

I,
Righteously,
For gods' sake,
Declare a holy war,
Condemn
The nonbeliever
In his hell
Belabour him, until
He comes to love me
As himself.

EIGHTY CANDLES

Hope burns.
Crescendo rhythms.
Ambition
sets torches,
lights the universe
until
accelerating time
slips by,
dribbles through fingers
spread too wide
to catch the moon.

Pan-pipe diminuendo.
Age quenches flames,
unfetters dreams,
flies high
above congealing time.
Then,
embers glowing,
wiser hands stretch out
beyond the rocking chair
to hold the sun.

PHOTO ALBUM

The cover says,
'My Family', in gold
And overleaf
– Page One –
A nest of wedding snaps.

Overleaf

Early years;
Sea, sun–seasons
And over, leaf on leaf,
Babies.
Play times.
Children
Swing on swings
And grow.

And overleaf,

In black and white,
Age waves farewell
from fair ground
Roundabouts.

But overleaf

Youth rides
The skelter run,
Sports
A handlebar moustache.
Young faces framed,
Unfixed,
Against a sepia sky.

And overleaf?

Memory is softer,
Gentle.
Joy nestles pain;
Mountain and valley soothed
To hard transparency.

AS ONE DOOR CLOSES

1

Dread curtains drawn. An open parlour door.
Barbed spears of cypress patterning the floor.
Three generations gathered at the gate.
A petal curls beside an empty grate.
Motes float in sunbeams, spotlight frozen time;
forget–me–nots in triptych silvered frame;

a wedding group, squint–eyed against the light,
pale sepia distilled from black and white.
Ghost images, three children, indistinct
seek recognition in a washed–out print.
A 'proper picture' taking pride of place,
four generations form the centre–piece.

2

Birds sing in gardens of secluded hours
where spring soothes winter's memory with flowers,
and solemn tocsins echo obsequies
where pansies sigh in scent of rosemary.
Motes float on sunbeams from the laurel wreath
where doors are closed and grass grows over grief.

DISTANCE REVISITED

I think he liked me, but
we were never close. I mean,
I never held my father's hand
or kissed him as a child.
We rarely talked but, screened
behind tobacco smoke, conversed
as if we had just met; polite,
a stranger sort of interest.
He'd not congratulate success,
nor slate more frequent failures, yet,
when he was ill, I raced again for him,
at school lapped through his mind
until the coma passed and, once more
crisis closed the gate.

Just now I found the cuttings;
wallet pockets of reviews, reports,
awards of prizes I had won or lost;
a yellowed catalogue of dreams
crumbled by silence. Outdistanced now
I kiss his cheek, listen to advice
he never gave in fifty years, sometimes
I hold his hand, discuss old principles;
fashioned standards he had set himself.
A quiet man of courage; but
valour failed to break a privacy
we could not share until today.

TAP ROOTS

Love rooted, planted where the balsam grows;
a sapling burgeoned in the may–flower leys
or, lissome, lashed by storms in darker days
will bow and bend before the harshest blows.

The cankered bough; a promise built on lies.
Doubt winnows doubt, a sly, exacted tithe
when passion frosts beneath the reaper's scythe,
and great oaks crumble when the tap root dies.

NINETY-ONE TODAY

We all sing Happy Birthday at her. Shrouded
In the greatcoat warmth of dreams, she watches
Out of tune with time, half comprehending
Half withdrawn into a children's world; asleep
Before she blows her candle out.

She talks to mother, teachers, friends in Praze*
Of chapel tea–treats' wicked innocence; Sun days,
God and saffron buns and sand, tea and teasing
Her dear Eddie of the dreaming teens; snuffed
On the Somme. 'For king and country. R.I.P.'

"Ten pennyworth of meat a week," she says,
Dusting the rubble of a Hitler bomb,
"And now he's broken mother's vase, the sod,
And killed poor Mrs Day," – dead fifty years –
"Lives for her garden, bless her heart."

We stand to, wish her well,
Toast her battle weary years, and she,
Deep in the dugout of her mind
Head safely down behind closed eyes
Reviews the march past of her age. "This year
The flowers are beautiful," she says.

* *a village in Cornwall*

Dragons lurk. In blue forests
giants prowl, stride seven leagues,
where hound packs quarter; dogs
with saucer eyes that watch;
waiting
for the eyelids' droop,
to pounce and come
hunting home.

Priests prey. In white flax–lands,
the Rumpelstiltskin prelates
plead virtue's worth, intone
their several requiems,
watching;
for the eyelids' close,
to gnaw at souls
hunted home.

CAST OFF

Cast off. You sound the depths of each reluctant breath
and strain to loose the tensioned, sickbed sheet. Unmoored,
wild fancies flit from darkened caverns of dead years
to lose their way in the distracted light. Cast off,

let slip dead springs and cut the cord a second time,
the time is now to sail beyond the shipwreck reefs.
Shrouded, bare-pole beyond slow-sweeping, look-out eyes
life gently drifts in Dis-dark Erewhon, on watch

cries landfall of the distant port. Long fingers point,
frail framework hands pluck at a ragged silence, stretch
from willowed shallows at the urgent river's edge,
to hold a death that missed the ferryman. At peace

you smile to recognise the pilot and his craft.
From Lethe's watermeadow berth take passage then
to sleep past sleep, released at last. Now shoot the sun,
unshackled, free, race downstream in the river's run.

SCAPE

I dream long hours when all the sky is pink.
Drowsers, we ramble in the blue flower fields
down–land and snow drift hand to hand, re–chart
the languid, secret boundaries, unfathomed
landscapes reflecting sunlight to the sea,
smooth tender treasure of the barrow mound
and tongue tied sip the moonglow tiger balm.
We map the coastline at our fingertips,
cast off, ride whitefoam crests and berth
in slumberous harbours to discover peace;
cradle heartsease for our willow days.

BLOOMING KIDS

They lie wide-eyed in sleep.
The nipple thumb milks dreams
Of chocolate trolls and roundabouts,
Of white maned horses snorting fire
That blaze across wide sands, loins
Flecked with foam, to swoop and sweep them
Into ecstasy, or rocket them to stars
Of Pop and space and television screen,
To score wild goals of unimagined bliss
That stamp the vital game with victory.
In innocence they dream of sin
As old as yesterdays.

STORMY WHETHER

Iceberg;
You awake
Distanced. Cold
Between glacier sheets.

Playboy;
I, asleep,
Venture out.
Dreaming heroic oats.

I may be gone some time.

WALK IN THE RAIN

We walk. You show me things I had not seen;
quick–sands, a star, sundews, a cloud and there
a beetle marching underneath my foot.

I stay my step to watch him scurry by
unruffled by the imminence of death.
His world revolves around a speck of dung;

his remnant from a greater good. Crouching
I watch his busy, slow parade, and turn
to see the boot above my head.

STRAINED RELATIONS

Cold, moonlight through the diamond panes
floods on her gold, her silver and her jewels,
and moonbeams splinter on his tinsels of success:
but it is shadowed where the true cost lies.

It is her slow nocturnal pat upon his back
that tells the truth behind her, "Never mind,"
and smiles that do not reach sad, empty eyes
that watch the wall and dream and fill with tears.

It is truth that cries, when silent pain
corrodes the certainty, and doubt sets seed
to root in fertile ground. It is truth that lies
with, "Doesn't matter," and her pat upon his back.

PRIMARY LESSON

They taught,
"If you spin a rainbow
painted on a top,
the rainbow's colours
turn to white."
They did not teach
that time spins colour
at the rainbow's end
to black.

BED

Double, king size, yet
too small. You always
encroached; tapping warmth
occupied my space, explored
with feet of ice.

Single king size now,
an arctic desert
stretching beyond fingertips
that probe the future
seeking the past.

REQUIESCAT

Love me gentle, gentle maiden
Couch me, snugly, in your heart.
Let the May times be remembered,
Storms remaindered when we part.

Sleep me still in timeless slumber;
Years the peace of loving span,
Let no anguished spirit wander
Through the memories of man.

Breathe my dreamland into living
With the perfumed breath of life,
Death is but a new beginning
Endless freedom without strife.

Sweet the bourn that we encompass,
Blest the meeting of our ways,
The immortal We is with us
To our children's children's days.

Days of age to youthful pleasure
So the roundabout goes round.
Every man is his own future
Every man for ever bound.

THERE YOU ARE

I hear your footsteps
on the pavement of my mind
and turning
hear your laughter in the hills
your sorrows
in the buzzard's cry

A quiet love
pressed
in the laundered shirt
trapped
in a spider's web of thread

FAMILY GARDEN

At coffee time I sit and, through the window,
Watch feeding swallows stutter in the air,
Parade of doves, a slow turn of daisies
As shadows shorten when the morning dies.

My grandson in the garden of my days
Plays on my swing, still there. Discarded toys,
The bric a brac of children, fill the space.
Where lupins blossomed; now a swimming pool.

Hard shadows in the garden, black with light,
Lengthen as birdsong makes the silence loud.
A scythe swoops, hissing at lank grass
Lays hope to parch in regimented ranks.

Bed time. I take my stick to stroll at dusk.
Birds chat in trees. The scythe sings louder now.
Reflections in blind windows of the house –
We ramble in the garden of long days.

LEFTOVERS

A remnant picnic on a peak, above the beach
where young-days trickle out through hourglass hands
and dancing footsteps tread the measured pace
from sprightly galop to the slow pavane.

The prance of foot-prints halts in shifting sand.
High time marks time at spring-tide edge of seas
where foam-back horses buck, retreat and plunge
to siren singing and the sob of waves.

At twilight turn, to see in silhouette
refurbished tables set against the sun
and silence, drowning moons in wrack-swept pools,
reflects night-dark on expurgated strands.

FRAME OF MIND

Monet reflections in the river's runs
calm seas and heaven, scumble–edged, conjoin
where silent tide–tongues kiss the dunes
beyond the mud flats and the curlew song,
and distant shapes with burgeoned spectral sails
whisper my dreams to lands of harsher grails;

mad Miro magic floating throught the mind
hot days of yellow sun on Douane cool,
tumultuous turquoise seas on silver sand,
star–studded skies of prussian blue.
These are my Gauguin lands of cloudless skies,
swirled scarlet skirts afloat on golden thighs.

Shackled, against grey canvas of long days,
we savour leisured hours of muted hues
bright pinpoint pleasures of a Seurat glaze,
and then Braque–broken truth intrudes.
In Dali worlds, where nothing's what it seems,
time bends – we sleep upon the death of dreams.

THE EVENING BEFORE WATERLOO
(The Duchess of Richmond's Ball)

Beyond the formal garden the redoubt.
Unnatural silence shrouds the distant lines,
While in the room soft candle lights shine out
On panoply the monarch's jewel defines.
To music's beat prance dancers up and down
Coy fans and eyelids flutter, "What delight
Invite him Mama, to our ball in Town."
Long sighs drown out the hoofbeat in the night.
"There is a harsher measure I must tread.
Forgive me Madam, I must ride away
Forsake the treasured pleasures of your bed
And pray that we may dance another day."
Now drummer drum, band play a different tune
For dancing men whose dancing days are done.

NORTH OF AMIENS

No old trees here: tall stands that sigh
In summer heat where meadows dance
And swooping meet a misting sky
Where valleys grey in Northern France.

Cows browsing crop these lusher leas
The bonemeal fields; rough plough-tip's bite
Turns Yorick skulls; fresh furrow frees
Young 'old-hands' lost that stretch for light.

A shell-case gleams near infants' cots,
Bright mirrored sun where children play,
Fresh blossoms flow from helmet pots
New flowers to dress a richer clay,

But tendrils twine, dead years, regrets
Guyed to rusted bayonets.

TOCCATA AND FUGUE

I have the sound of pictures in my mind;
paintstrokes on my imagination, coloured
cobble–blocks of sound, in ivory and black,
that rise and fall, by fingered steps,
along a sad notation of well–beaten tracks.
Tone deaf, the natural calls the tune
to score the elephant ephemeral as the chord
and, in the whirling season's carnival,
transposes harmony to a cavalcade of war.
There, horse and sheep unite and, at a stroke,
cry heartbreak on a fiddle string. There man,
on sacrificial hides, beats glory's hour;
on virgin parchment taps accelerating time
to glean the maypole's promise on a muffled drum.

PRIZE DAY

My Miss, Miss Searle
was tiny even then
when coathooks beckoned
high above my head.

Start–rite feet did not
quite reach
under historic desks;
names scrawled on lids
by birthday penknives
and black Stephens ink.

"Present Miss."

Names from long ago
fall in;
line up
in order;
answer at roll call.

This present Miss is tiny too.
Those coathook rows still stand
now no higher than my waist.
On knee–tall desks,
and on the wall,
the names remain.

"Present arms."

Those names
answered the Roll Call;
on orders
line up
in white–cross crocodiles.

REMEMBRANCE DAY PARADE

Courage, they say, is overcoming fear.
It is the hallmark of the manly breast
but widows, mourn and shed a bitter tear.

The brave lie buried tier on tier on tier
who, colours flying, passed the crucial test.
Courage, they say, is overcoming fear

of death that passed the thinning line each year
who march and mind for comrades now at rest;
but widows mourn, and shed a bitter tear.

"Reverse arms." Pomp cries, "Decorate the bier,"
then "Order arms." Ignore the bitter jest.
Courage, they say, is overcoming fear

The loss of face or status held so dear.
They cry for guns with undiminished zest
but widows mourn and shed a bitter tear.

Priests raise the cross and wave the flag and cheer.
Praise gods. Declaim the battle slain are blest.
Courage, they say, is overcoming fear;
but widows mourn and shed a bitter tear.

LIVING ROOM (1990)

What will you do in the *last* war, Daddy,
In desert fields that crop memorial fruit;
When white ash fingers point
Where whirlwinds spiral children's dust
And dry-sac women crouch where feral
Men take arms for lebensraum
Shadowed from sun?

BATTLEFIELD

Not far from Bagshot,
So refined,
They called the Home
'DUNROMIN'.
Tactless sods.

Wrought iron gates.
Delphinium guards.
Parade ground lawns
Short back and sides.
This lot've done with roaming,
Poor old dears
Confined to barracks.
Jankered.

Wheel-chaired,
Under the cedar tree,
They march through Alamein, or drop
Like thistle seeds
To glory.

Striped tie, blazer, regimental crest.
You can see the weathered face reflect
In Church's shoes.
Poor Old Buggers. Gift-wrapped
In tartan rugs, they chew the fat;
On toothless gums re-savour banquets
Of the junior mess.
All day they think of tea,
Or nothing.

Stand easy.

Beside another cedar tree,
Just far enough away,
The twin-set widows knit,
Play bridge, stir memories
Borne on east wind tiles; Mah Jong,
and those "Do you remember days?"

Wrinkled,
Ramrod,
In majesty,
Just far enough apart,
Alexandra Parker-Brown
The solitary Mem,
Reads Books.

Bugle sounds
Retreat.

'DUNROMIN'.
Tactless sods.
Might just as well be
'AFTERLIFE'.

TIME EXPOSURE

Saved in the grey museum, locked from light,
Soft swaddling tissues shroud a sepia ghost,
A swirling copperplate of rusted ink:
'Street. 1868. - Daguerreotype.'

Fruitery. Bakery. Grocery. Cobbler.
Fishmonger. Milliner. Ironmonger. Butcher,
A shopper's street of bustle, dung and smells,
The death of pigs priced clearly on white tags.
Lines rim the edge of stones in dark;
Hard shadows narrowed by the time of day.

The fading slow-march of their cavalcade?
The camera warps the tapestry of trade;
Even the pedlar's sluggard pace too fast
To leave his trail on sluggish silver film.

The living street is lost. No housewives stop
To shop for gossip and the evening meal.
No children play. No straining horses braced
Against the foison of the merchants' carts.

Today's daguerreotype?
A filtered film of gold behind the eyes.
We watch our hubbub helter-skelter world
Too slow to recognise the humdrum's worth;
Our unrecorded 'now' a Din too fast
To leave an image in the future's frame.

MARKET WOMAN

Past stalls the market river flows, currents,
shoppers and watchers, ebb and flow; eddies
without sharp angles, never touch, never
ruffle on her shores. She browses finger tips
through spider-webbing harmonies of lace.

Long time. I watch. She stands beside the Sorgue,
an island-calm in crowd-flow, set apart;
this solitaire in ectoplasmic white,
a slender shade in harsh Provençal noon.
She hides her face behind a cart-wheel hat.

I picture beauty there. Serenity
shadow and light perfection, secret, veiled
beyond a brim. But if she would turn her head...
I long to see. Enigma, only turn...
but, still behind her brim, she walks away.

I'll picture beauty there. Serenity
shadow and light perfection, secret, veiled.

THE SURGEON
(For Mike)

Laconic he, the Renal Man, had seen it all
the 'Plumbing Failures', and the end
before our transplant days, when death
is dialysed away three times a week.
Coiled in a wrinkled leather chair
that wrapped him like a mother's arms
he read memorial columns in the Times
as if he knew he was a short haul fare.
"I always look," he used to say, "just check
to see if my name's there. If not, well then,
I know it's safe to go and start my day."

Today it listed, 'Kidney failure, bravely borne,
Beloved son. Aged thirty five.' "Typical."
his spirit seems to say, "What bloody luck,
and bravely borne, my arse!"

WHEELS OF INDUSTRY

Full circle turning, circling, turned around
this naked captain in the six foot cot,
who, mewling, spirit rubbed and nappy bound,
relives the journey to his penthouse slot.

This naked captain in the six foot cot
climbs from the breadline to a boardroom height,
relives the journey to his penthouse slot,
accepts success with unconcealed delight;

climbs from the breadline to a boardroom height,
and holding industry within his grip
accepts success with unconcealed delight
signing the contract with his finger's tip

and holding industry within his grip
squeezes his foes, and then invokes a clause
signing the contract with his finger's tip
 – Please God, ignore my inadvertant flaws. –

squeezes his foes, and then invokes a clause,
crying for mother and the milky breast,
"Please God ignore my inadvertant flaws."
His millstone wheel of fortune grinds to rest.

The cashiered captain, now all lessons learned,
who mewling, spirit rubbed and nappy bound,
completes the barefoot round – all bridges burned
full circle turning, circling, turned around.

POET AND PEASANT

The study of science, he said, is sublime
But marriage of science and art is a crime.
For Science is Science and Art is, well, art
They don't go together so keep them apart.

Sad! I considered, you poor philistine.

We study facts purely, but poets play tricks
Thus proving that science and art cannot mix.
That's rot, I replied, why not give it a try
Some poetry's wierd, but some's easy as pie.

I'll show you, I said, if you have the time.

Take, 'pie', for instance. Let your memory roam
To savour, to sniff it, to carry you home
To kneadings and rollings and bakings of bread.
Remember those pastries and fillings? I said.

Now here's a scansion change, and shortened line.

Short, tempered, golden crust on apple pulp
Or, rough-puffed macho pie of beef-steak hulk
- Free-standing, piping hot - and topless tart;
Spice-scented steam revealed the rose's heart?

Note change of rhythm. Note internal rhyme.

Let sights and sounds and smell of pies
Roll off your pen of ecstasies;
And sigh and dream what might have been.
Pie in the sky. See what I mean?

You try. I remarked, you'll manage just fine.

O.K., he said, there is, all said and done,
Great beauty in the concept of a pi
Where 3.142 runs on and on
As numbers trudge towards infinity.

You mean that sort of thing? he said. The swine.

Based on an article which suggested that the disciplines of poetry and science were mutually exclusive.

Gourmet, she savours plagues and illnesses,
gathers their signs and symptoms, clutches them
to hatch and peck at fears, a miser's hoard
rich, secret, treasure-deep in dungeon mind.
She holds court in her doctor's waiting room.
Each Thursday is her day; to harvest doom,
winnow the crop, sow subtle seeds of doubt,
take turn to reconfirm the ignorance
– of local quacks.

"Hallo, and how are you, my dear?" you say.
A greeting to the day? No, it's the key
that opens flood gates of her constant pains,
intrepid agonies that knot and grind,
"Scalding," throughout her long and sleepless nights,
"Stabbing, right through;"
her endless nightmare days.
"Such agony," she moans, "I always say,
'I'm rooted, like that crippled Benson girl
– but so much worse.'

Of course, I have to try to carry on,
I wonder how I manage with the pain.
Friends say, 'How brave,' but, as I always say,
'One simply has to try. I do my best.'
Is that the time? My dear, such fun to chat,
must absolutely fly, I'm first on tee;
starting the morning round (if spared) at eight, it
will be Hell, but as I always say...One simply has..."

STONE DEAF

Blinded by silence
poetry uncoloured music
muted
rhythms beat
out of step
words silenced
syllables
vent feelings
without emotion
a marionette world
paying lip service.

THE SECRET

Tenderness, love–locked
in marble: rough hewn
until the chisel tap
released The Kiss –

sniggering, the crocodile
files past:
reduces form to
        What a pair of tits,
the master's touch to
        Watch 'is 'and, the sods
        are all the same.
But

one or two
see beauty
hand–picked.

ENID

Enid as a blushing schoolgirl
Tapioca oft eschewed
Thinking, in her genteel fashion
Its appearance rather rude.

Times have changed and so has Enid
Now her thoughts are strange and lewd.
Now her joys are somewhat curious
Involving sago, in the nude.

THE G.P. IF

If you can keep your health when all about you
Are losing theirs and blaming it on you.
If you control yourself when all reps tout you
Yet make allowance of their touting too.
If you can fill each unfulfilling minute
With ninety seconds worth of instant hope,
And view the Ministry and everyone that's in it
And yet not murmur, "Just a bit more rope."
If you can face the world with Jobian patience,
And offer more when there's no more to give.
Then you will have an endless list of patients,
But watch it mate, you're too damned good to live.